D1553576

THE ULTIMATE

Penguin

Book for Kids

100+ Penguin Facts, Photos, Quiz and More

BELLANOVA

MELBOURNE · SOFIA · BERLIN

ISBN: 9798420673034
Independently Published

CONTENTS

*Two King penguins
and their chick.*

INTRODUCTION

It's hard not to love penguins! But how much do you really know about your favorite cold weather-loving bird?

In this book you will learn over 100 amazing new things about penguins—from Emperors to Adeliés. You'll be a penguin expert in no time.

Are you ready? Let's go!

Emperor penguin with a chick >

PENGUIN
FACTS

Penguins are flightless birds. They can only walk and swim.

• • •

Most penguins live in the Southern Hemisphere.

• • •

Penguins don't only live in cold climates. There are large penguin populations in countries including Australia, New Zealand, South Africa and Chile.

King penguins standing close to an Antarctic fur seal.

Even though it's salty, penguins are able to drink sea water.

• • •

There are no penguins living at the North Pole.

• • •

The Galapagos penguin is only one type of penguin that naturally heads north of the equator.

Falkland Island penguins.

Magellanic penguins in Patagonia.

Falkland Island penguins

Most penguins are not sexually dimorphic, meaning both the males and females look the same.

Penguins may look like they have wings, but they only use them as flippers to swim.

• • •

Emperor penguins are able to stay underwater for up to 20 minutes at a time.

• • •

Penguins spend around half of their life in the water and the other half on land.

When penguins that live in Antarctica are on land, they have no predators. Their only predators are in the sea.

. . .

Wild penguins typically live for 15-20 years.

. . .

Because they have no natural land predators, penguins are generally not afraid of humans.

The Emperor penguin is the tallest species of penguin. They can be as tall as 47 inches (120 cm).

• • •

Penguins lost their ability to fly millions of years ago. Now they are the fastest swimming and deepest diving birds on the planet.

• • •

Fossils show that the earliest species of penguins lived over 60 million years ago. That means that ancestors of the penguins we see today survived the extinction of the dinosaurs.

Penguins have a special gland behind their eyes — the **supraorbital gland** — that filters out saltwater from their bloodstream. The salt is then excreted through their beaks or by sneezing.

. . .

A **rookery** is where penguins mate, nest and raise their chicks.

. . .

Chinstrap penguins have been nicknamed 'stonecracker penguins' due to their exceptionally loud cries.

Gentoo penguins with chicks.

Yellow-eyed penguins have bright yellow eyes like cats. They are the third largest species of penguin in the world.

. . .

Little Blue penguins are the smallest species of penguin, they average around 13 inches (33 cm) in height.

. . .

Crested penguins have yellow crests as well as red eyes and bill.

Chinstrap penguin >

Rockhopper penguins in Argentina.

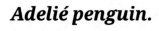

Adelié penguin.

When it gets very cold in Antarctica, Emperor penguins often huddle together to stay warm.

. . .

There are 17 species of penguins, 13 of which are endangered or on the brink of extinction.

. . .

Penguins often enter the sea in large groups. Scientists believe this is to ensure safety in numbers.

Yellow-eyed penguins are native to New Zealand. They are endangered and there are only around 4000 still living in the wild, making them the rarest penguins in the world.

. . .

Do you know why penguins are black and white? It helps to camouflage them in the water. The black on their backs is hard to see from above, while the white on the front looks like the sun reflecting off the water when seen from below.

Yellow-eyed penguins.

In relation to the size of the animal, penguin eggs are the smallest of any bird species. Also, their egg shells are much thicker than most other eggs, which helps protect them in the harsh environment.

• • •

Most species of penguins lay two eggs at a time. However, Emperor and King penguins don't build a nest and lay a single egg.

• • •

Penguins aren't the only flightless birds. Others include kiwis, ostriches, cassowaries, emus and rheas.

A King penguin.

Chinstrap penguins in Antarctica.

Chinstrap penguins get their name from the thin black line that circles under their chin. They are one of the most aggressive breeds of penguin.

• • •

Baby penguins are called chicks.

• • •

Approximately 1 in 50,000 penguins are born with a brown plumage instead of black. These are called Isabelline penguins, and they tend to live shorter lives than black penguins because they aren't able to camouflage as well.

Emperor penguins

Emperor penguin chicks.

African penguins.

A group of penguin chicks is called a **créche**.

• • •

Have you seen the movie *Happy Feet*? The main penguins in the movie are Emperor penguins.

• • •

The **Gentoo penguin** is the fastest underwater swimming bird. It can reach speeds of up to 22 mph (36 km/h).

Penguins often slide their bodies along ice and snow. This is called tobogganing. It is believed they do this both for fun and to get places faster.

• • •

A group of penguins in the water is called a raft. A group of penguins on the land is called a waddle.

• • •

Penguins find all of their food in the sea. They mostly eat fish and squid and a large penguin can catch up to 30 fish in one dive.

Emperor penguins and their chicks >

Gentoo penguins.

Penguins can swim three times faster than they can walk on land.

• • •

Penguins pant like dogs when they are too hot to help them cool off.

• • •

Penguins don't have teeth. Instead, they use their beaks to grab onto their prey. They also have spikes on their tongue that helps with extra grip.

Falkland Island penguins.

Rockhopper penguins.

When penguins eat, they also swallow pebbles and stones. Scientists think that this is to help them digest their food. Another theory is that the stones help weigh the penguins down so that they can dive deeper.

• • •

King penguins create nesting colonies of up to 10,000 penguins.

• • •

Emperor penguins breed in the coldest environment of all penguin species. The air temperature can be as cold as -40° F (-40° C)

African penguin colony at the beach in South Africa.

Penguins swim so fast that they can propel themselves through water and cut through waves just like dolphins can. The technique they use is called **porpoising**.

• • •

Small penguins tend to live in temperate climates such as Australia and South America, while large penguins live in the cooler climates such as Antarctica.

When penguin chicks are born they are not waterproof, meaning they have to be careful to stay out of the water. They rely on their parents to bring them food and keep them warm.

. . .

Some prehistoric penguins could grow as tall and heavy as humans!

. . .

Only two species of penguins live in Antarctica — Emperor penguins and the Adélie penguin.

A macaroni penguin.

A fear of penguins is called sphenisciphobia. But we assume you don't have that!

• • •

Macaroni penguins get their name from the long, orange, yellow and black feathery crests they have above their eyes.

• • •

Penguins have better eyesight underwater than they do on land.

Penguins cannot breathe underwater. However, they can stay underwater for 10-20 minutes before they need to come up to breathe.

. . .

King penguins, the second largest species of penguin, don't waddle like most penguins do—they run quite quickly on their feet.

. . .

Penguins are very sociable. They do most things in groups both on land and in water.

Gentoo penguins coming ashore.

A huge penguin colony on Bird Island, Patagonia.

Gentoo penguins.

The normal body temperature of most penguins is 100° F (38° C).

• • •

Penguins lose their feathers, or molt, once a year. When they have lost their feathers they are no longer waterproof, so they need to wait until their feathers grow back before they can go back into the water. During this time, which can take weeks, penguins can lose up to half their body weight.

• • •

Penguins spend several hours a day preening their feathers. This is very important, as it keeps them waterproof.

Penguins spread oil, which comes from a gland near their tail feathers, onto their feathers to provide extra waterproofing.

. . .

The most common threats to penguins in the wild are pollution, commercial fishing, oil dumping and global warming.

. . .

The Galapagos penguin has lost over 50% of its species since the 1970's. Scientists estimate they have a 30% chance of becoming extinct this century if they are not protected.

King penguins.

King penguins.

There are two days a year to celebrate penguins! January 20 is *Penguin Awareness Day*, while April 25 is *World Penguin Day*. How will you celebrate?

. . .

Every year, the world's population of Adelié penguins eats around 1.5 million metric tons of krill! On top of that, they also eat squid and fish.

. . .

Most penguin species are monogamous. They don't always have the same partner throughout their life, however, they only have one partner during each mating season.

Emperor penguin chicks in South Georgia.

Overfishing of the oceans by humans
takes away food from penguins
and is causing a decrease in many
species.

. . .

Emperor penguins incubate their
eggs by keeping them warm on top of
their feet. Underneath a featherless
fold of skin there are lots of blood
vessels that keep the egg warm.

Little penguins.

A Humboldt penguin.

Both penguin parents, male and female, take care of their young for several months until the chicks are strong enough to hunt for their own food.

. . .

If a female Emperor penguin's chick dies, she will often "kidnap" another chick.

. . .

Penguins have knees. The upper parts of their legs are covered by feathers.

Most sea mammals rely on blubber to keep them warm underwater. Penguins, on the other hand, survive because their feathers trap a layer of warm air next to their skin that provides insulation.

· · ·

Scientists have discovered that the color of penguin poop varies depending on their diet. The more krill they eat, the pinker their droppings are.

· · ·

Most species of penguins are loyal to their nesting site. They will often return to the same rookery they were born in to lay their eggs.

PENGUIN QUIZ

Now test your knowledge in the Penguin Quiz! Answers can be found on page 75.

1 What is the largest species of penguin?

2 What food do penguins mostly eat?

3 Where do penguins live?

4 Which animal group do penguins belong to?

5 How many species of penguin are there?

King penguins

6   What is the smallest species of penguin?

7   Why are penguins' nests located above sea level?

8   How do penguins often move across the ice?

9   How do penguins swim in the water?

10   How deep can an Emperor penguin dive?

11   When do penguins eat?

12   What makes the Emperor penguins breeding habits unique?

13   How does the Emperor penguin incubate its egg in Antarctica?

14 Can penguins breathe underwater?

15 Penguins have knees. True or false?

16 What do you call a group of penguins in the water?

17 What are baby penguins called?

18 What is one of the biggest threats to penguins?

19 On which date is *World Penguin Day* celebrated?

Emperor penguin with a chick.

ANSWERS

1. Emperor penguins
2. Krill, squid and fish
3. Only in the southern hemisphere
4. Birds
5. 17
6. Little blue penguin
7. To keep them safe from seals
8. They glide across the ice on their stomachs
9. They swim with their wings while using their feet as rudders
10. 1,700 feet (736m)
11. Only when they are at sea
12. The male incubates the egg the whole time
13. On top of its feet
14. No
15. True
16. A raft
17. Chicks
18. Overfishing by humans
19. April 25

Penguin
WORD SEARCH

```
F G A D E L I E E X H V
G E H G F F S N F Z X B
R U M W I Y I V R D S E
E Y Y P R E S C V C S A
S R T F E A T H E R S K
D S E B H R Q W V G F S
B F G F D S O B V C Z W
H F L I P P E R N T D G
F K R P E N G U I N S T
S I G B G D S W K U F J
A N T A R C T I C A G H
V G Q W R G F S P E R F
```

Can you find all the words below in the word search puzzle on the left?

EMPEROR   ICE   BEAK

ANTARCTICA   KING   FLIPPER

FEATHERS   PENGUINS   ADELIE

SOLUTION

	A	D	E	L	I	E				
	E								B	
		M		I					E	
			P		C				A	
		F	E	A	T	H	E	R	S	K
				R						
					O					
	F	L	I	P	P	E	R			
	K		P	E	N	G	U	I	N	S
	I									
A	N	T	A	R	C	T	I	C	A	
	G									

SOURCES

Penguins, 10. 2022. **"10 Cool Facts About Penguins"**. *City Of Albuquerque.* https://www.cabq.gov/artsculture/biopark/news/10-cool-facts-about-penguins.

"Penguin - Wikipedia". 2022. *En.Wikipedia. Org.* https://en.wikipedia.org/wiki/Penguin.

"Penguin Facts". 2022. Greenpeace.Org.Uk. https://www.greenpeace.org.uk/news/penguin-facts/.

"Fun Facts About Penguins! - Cool Australia". *Cool Australia.* 2012. https://www.coolaustralia.org/fun-facts-about-penguins/.

"Emperor Penguin - Wikipedia". 2022. *En.Wikipedia.Org.* https://en.wikipedia.org/wiki/Emperor_penguin.

"30 Fascinating Facts About Penguins That Prove Just How Majestic (And Adorable) They Are". 2020. *Good Housekeeping.* https://www.goodhousekeeping.com/life/g19844807/penguin-facts/.

"5 Fun Penguin Facts | SEA LIFE Sydney Aquarium". 2022. *SEA LIFE Sydney Aquarium.* https://www.visitsealife.com/sydney/information/news/5-fun-facts-about-penguins/.

"30 Fun Penguin Facts For Kids You'll Wish You'd Known | Earth Eclipse". 2022. *Earth Eclipse.* https://eartheclipse.com/animals/penguin-facts-for-kids.html.

"A Phylogenomic Study Of Birds Reveals Their Evolutionary History". 2022. *Science.* https://www.science.org/doi/10.1126/science.1157704.

"Penguins Of Australia And New Zealand". 2022. *Web.Archive.Org.* https://web.archive.org/web/20120217205921/http://www.siec.k12.in.us/west/proj/penguins/australia.html.

We hope you learnt some awesome facts about
penguins!

We'd love it if you wrote us a review — it always makes us smile, and it helps other readers make better decisions about their next read.

*Visit us at
www.bellanovabooks.com
for more great books and giveaways!*

ALSO BY JENNY KELLETT

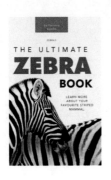  

... and more!

AVAILABLE IN ALL MAJOR BOOKSTORES

Made in the USA
Columbia, SC
15 December 2022

6a90002b-cb8b-4fcf-958a-6353669289b6R01